Original title:
Life: It's What You Make of It (But No Pressure)

Copyright © 2025 Creative Arts Management OÜ
All rights reserved.

Author: Penelope Hawthorne
ISBN HARDBACK: 978-1-80566-166-5
ISBN PAPERBACK: 978-1-80566-461-1

The Quiet Power of Dreams

In a world that's loud and bright,
Your dreams can take their flight.
Whispers turning into roars,
Watch them open up the doors.

Pajamas on, late-night snack,
Dreams dance 'round, no looking back.
If a unicorn can take a dive,
Who says you can't feel alive?

Mosaic of the Mundane

Sock puppets sing in the hall,
Every trip's a playful sprawl.
Dishes laugh while they are spun,
Mundane? Nah, it's all in fun.

Coffee spills like morning cheer,
Each little mess speaks out clear.
Shake the routine, break the mold,
Life's a canvas, bright and bold.

Finding Joy in the Journey

Missed the bus, but found a cat,
Wanderlust in a chatty hat.
Every corner hides a giggle,
Bumps in the road, just a wiggle.

Aimless paths and silly slips,
Dancing snacks on fingertips.
Take a step, then take a chance,
Joy's a partner in this dance.

The Alchemy of Aspirations

Hopscotch dreams and paper planes,
Glitter clouds and joyful rains.
Mixing hopes like salted fries,
Sprinkling magic in our pies.

Dreams, like cookies, need some dough,
Knead them well, let them grow.
Turn the mundane into spark,
Every moment, leave a mark.

Threads of Tomorrow

I stitched my dreams with colored thread,
Each knot a laugh, not a little dread.
With scissors poised and mischief in sight,
I cut the worries, let the fun take flight.

The future's fabric is quirky and bright,
With design flaws that spark pure delight.
A patchwork of moments, both silly and grand,
I wear my creations with a wink and a hand.

Sunshine through the Windows

When life gives clouds, I paint them yellow,
With sunbeams shining on each little hello.
I hang my hat on a sunny ray,
And dance through raindrops in a froggy ballet.

Through windows wide, the laughter streams,
Like kids with ice cream and endless dreams.
The world's a circus, so grab a seat,
And take a sip of silly lemonade, oh sweet!

A Dance with Uncertainty

I twirl with doubt, a clumsy romance,
Each misstep's a part of the dance.
Waltzing with fears, I trip and I glide,
Making up moves like I'm on a joyride.

Between two left feet and a grin so wide,
I shuffle through worries, oh what a stride!
With rhythm of laughter, I spin through the night,
In a dance that's absurd, but feels just right.

Navigating the Open Sea

My boat's made of dreams, with sails of hope,
I paddle with laughter, not a need to cope.
The waves may wobble, they ebb and they flow,
But I steer with giggles, just letting it go.

Though storms may rumble with sounds quite absurd,
I'll dodge 'em with jokes, not a single word.
The ocean's vast, but my compass is clear,
Just follow the funny, and steer with good cheer.

The Symphony of Your Steps

Each footfall plays a quirky tune,
A clumsy dance beneath the moon.
When you trip and laugh with glee,
You find your rhythm, wild and free.

Turn missteps into playful pairs,
With silly moves, who really cares?
In this ballet so absurdly bright,
You're the star of this crazy night.

Sunlight on the Horizon

Morning rays peek through the blinds,
Chasing away the sleepy minds.
With a toast and a grin so wide,
You jump into the day, full of pride.

Crayon skies and pancake flips,
Syrup rivers and sunny trips.
Life's a party, join the fun,
Dance around until you're done.

Where Paths Converge

When paths collide, it's quite the scene,
Juggling dreams like a circus queen.
With every twist and every turn,
You find new tricks and things to learn.

Stumble upon an odd surprise,
A dancing cat or pizza pies.
In this mix, embrace the strange,
Each moment's wild; it's time to change.

The Tapestry of Your Day

Stitches of laughter, threads of cheer,
Weave the madness, bring it near.
Each knot a memory, bright and bold,
A patchwork story waiting to be told.

In the fabric of this funny quest,
Find pockets of joy; they're the best.
Hang out with mishaps, invite them in,
And wear your quirks like a silly grin.

Whispers of Possibility

A cat sat on a mat, so round,
Dreaming of cheese, no worries found.
The sun shone bright, a perfect day,
But what if it rained? Let's dance away!

A squirrel named Ned, oh what a sight,
Built a treehouse with not much might.
He laughed and he squeaked at the birds in flight,
Who said he could not? They just weren't right!

Tapestry of Choices

A juggler juggles with bananas and fries,
Asked what he wanted, he just sighs.
'Should I become a magician or fly?',
While throwing in pies that all make you cry.

A hamster on wheels spins better than most,
Dreams of the cheese, he'll dance and he'll toast.
With all of his friends, they join in a feast,
But let's be honest, it's not for the least.

The Symphony of Struggles

A frog on a log sang terribly loud,
Thought he was famous, was lost in the crowd.
The crickets just chuckled, joined in with glee,
'We'll form a band! Just wait and see!'

An elephant danced in a tutu bright,
With creatures around, oh what a sight!
Too big for the ballet, oh what a mess,
But who's going to judge? He's doing his best!

Kaleidoscope of Moments

A cow took a leap, oh what a fall,
'Was it the grass or my poor stall?'
She tumbled and spun, in the air she flew,
'Moo-vin' for glory, it's what I'll do!'

A snail on a quest, slow but so spry,
For dreams of the world, he reached for the sky.
With each little step, he just can't be beat,
In a race against time, he won't take a seat.

The Flicker of Genuine Joy

Wake up, stretch, hit the snooze,
Coffee spills, oh what a muse!
Chasing socks, they're on the run,
Laughing loudly, just for fun.

Baking cookies, what a mess,
Flour flying, oh I confess!
Burnt the batch, but that's okay,
Order pizza, hip-hip-hooray!

Dancing wildly, socks askew,
Who needs rhythm? Not my crew!
Each little giggle, fuels the day,
Joy's silly games, come out to play.

So here's to joy, messy and bright,
In the chaos, take your flight!
With every slip and every trip,
We find the joy, let laughter rip!

Seeds of Your Imagination

Plant a thought, watch it grow,
A dream sprouted from a toe!
Paint a canvas, splash and twirl,
Grow a garden in a whirl.

Riding unicorns, oh what flair,
Send a letter to the air!
Dance with shadows, sing with light,
In this world, everything's right.

Jump on clouds with a bouncy cheer,
Tell a llama, "You're my dear!"
Invent a game with no rule book,
Sneak a peek, come take a look.

Here's to your wild, wacky spree,
With dreams as big as the deep blue sea!
So plant your seeds, let's make it grand,
Imagination's fun, take a hand!

Terrain of Wonders

Crumbling roads and twisty paths,
Collect your laughs, forget the maths!
Potholes filled with chocolate fudge,
Drive through joy, no need to grudge.

Mountains made of marshmallow peaks,
Sumptuous valleys, where silliness peaks.
Giggling flowers, not a bore,
Let's cartwheel to the candy store!

Oceans splash with soda pop,
Dive right in, but don't you stop!
Surf the waves of crisp delight,
In this terrain, everything's right.

So gather round for endless thrills,
Explore the landscape of laughs and chills!
With each adventure, treat it bright,
This wondrous land is pure delight!

Echoes of Laughter

Whispers of giggles in the air,
Join the chorus, a merry flare!
Jokes tumble out like playful rain,
In a world where fun's the main.

Chasing echoes down the street,
Winging puns, oh what a feat!
Ticklish feet and silly poses,
Each little chuckle, life just dozes.

Distant chuckles, drawing near,
Bring the fun; let's make it clear!
Share a laugh, then take a bow,
In this moment, joy's here now!

So spin around, dance like a fool,
Silly antics, here's the rule!
In echoes bright, let laughter thrive,
This funny world, oh, how we jive!

Breaths of Confidence

A deep breath taken with flair,
I trip on my shoes, but who really cares?
With a wink and a grin, I'll strut my stuff,
Each stumble a dance, oh isn't that tough?

The mirror's laughing, it knows my game,
A hot mess, but I play for the fame.
Confidence from crumbs, that's what I bake,
In this circus of clumsiness, smiles I make.

Shadows and Silhouettes of What Could Be.

Chasing shadows in the midday sun,
Are they just whispers or the real fun?
In the corner of my eye, they play tricks,
Where could I be? Just a few little flicks!

Silhouettes laughing, they tease and they taunt,
Dancing around like I'm some sort of font.
What could it be, this blurry delight?
A riddle unwinding in the soft light.

In the Garden of Choices

In a garden where choices grow wild and free,
I pick a blue flower, but just wait and see.
A petal for laughter, a stem for a leap,
We'll water the dreams and sow what we keep.

With a hoe of humor, we toil in the soil,
Each choice planted right makes our hearts recoil.
Smiles blossom bright, even weeds can delight,
In this chaotic garden, everything feels right.

Beneath a Canopy of Dreams

Under dreams in the trees, I sit and I grin,
The fruit of my labor? A laugh and a spin.
Each leaf tells a story, of whimsy and cheer,
Climbing high just to mess with my fear.

The squirrels are judging my clumsy ballet,
But chirps of delight seem to cheer me each day.
Beneath this sweet canopy, nothing feels wrong,
Just a jig and a giggle, it's where I belong.

Sculpting Intentions

In the clay of dreams we mold,
Laughter echoes, stories told.
With every laugh, a shape we find,
A masterpiece, one of a kind.

Chasing whims, we twist and turn,
In bright ideas, our hearts will burn.
A little mess, a joyful spree,
Who knew creating could be so free?

Fingers stained with colors bold,
Like toddler artists, we break the mold.
Each silly giggle, a guiding tool,
In this grand art, we're all a fool!

Flickers of Innovation

The light bulb blinks with playful glee,
   Ideas dance like bees in spree.
With quirky thoughts that leap and bound,
   We find our joys on shaky ground.

Inventing worlds both wild and bright,
   Our goofy passions take their flight.
With a wink and wiggle, we start to play,
   In playful chaos, we find our way.

A toaster that sings, a fridge that hums,
   Our strange inventions make us chums.
So kick back, relax, and let it be,
   In this zany realm, we're ever free!

Harmonies of the Everyday

The whistle of the kettle sings,
As breakfast crumbles, laughter springs.
In the chaos of morning's rush,
We find the fun, the goofy hush.

Toothpaste flying, socks mismatched,
With every blunder, joy attached.
The playlist of our daily grind,
Has silly beats that make us unwind.

Each moment's rhythm, a quirky beat,
We dance through life on wobbly feet.
In simple acts, we find the song,
In our bumbling ways, we all belong.

The Pulse of Potential

A heartbeat skips with silly cheer,
As dreams pop up likearty balloons near.
With every beat, our hopes ignite,
In cackles and giggles, we take flight.

Oh, the magic in our odd mistakes,
Turns fumbles into quirky wakes.
With open hearts and crazy spins,
In this dance of chance, everyone wins!

Embrace the blunders, give them space,
For in the chaos, we find grace.
The pulse of fun, a vibrant thread,
Threads us together, laughs widely spread.

A Journey of Your Own Design

Pack your bags, grab a snack,
Adventure calls, no time to slack.
A map's just paper, online's just memes,
Dance to the tunes of your wildest dreams.

Step right up, it's your own show,
Twist and turn, just let it flow.
No need for a manual, no need for a chart,
Just follow your giggles, that's where you start.

Sometimes you trip, and that's okay,
Trip on a shoelace, then laugh all day.
With each quirky turn, a new friend's found,
Turn your mishaps into joy all around.

So leap with glee, no reason to frown,
You're the star, don't ever back down!
In this grand ride, it's a silly parade,
So grab your confetti, let's make it a charade!

The Palettes of Persistence

Splash some color on the gray,
Even if you paint it the wrong way.
Swirl and twirl, don't stick to the norm,
Your life's a canvas, just let it transform.

Doodles turn into masterpieces,
When you laugh through the smudges, all worries cease.
Each brushstroke's a giggle, a skip, a dance,
Embrace the chaos, give joy a chance.

With pastels of persistence, paint your days,
Mix up your colors in humorous ways.
Who needs perfection, that's such a bore,
Embrace the mess and shout, "More, more!"

So grab your brush, unleash the fun,
For this mad art piece has only begun.
Create your own tapestry, wild yet sincere,
In this colorful journey, there's nothing to fear!

Chasing the Unseen

What's that there, just out of sight?
A ghost, a unicorn, or just bad light?
Chasing shadows with no clear map,
Laughter echoes, let's share a laugh!

With binoculars on your face, oh dear,
Looking for treasures, sipping on cheer.
Is it a mirage or just a prank?
Follow those giggles, that's the perfect flank.

So leap into dreams, with all your might,
Chase the unseen, it's a wild flight.
Forget the worries, they can't catch you,
In this funny chase, you'll find something new.

Embrace the puzzlement, it's all a game,
Finding joy in each twist and turn, it's all the same.
Raise your binoculars, let's spot the fun,
The unseen is waiting, your adventure's begun!

Beyond the Blueprint

Blueprints scribbled in crayon and glee,
Plans are just puzzles from A to Z.
Draw a line here, but make it a loop,
Plans can wobble into the silliest scoop.

Wander off course, it's totally fine,
The detours are filled with a splash of wine.
Mistakes lead to laughter, that's how it goes,
So shake off the stress, feel free to doze.

Dance on the sidelines, twirl with glee,
Life isn't a straight line, it's a playful spree.
Erase the worries, add a pinch of cheer,
Your design's a giggle that draws everyone near.

So step off the blueprint, let ideas collide,
Who needs a straight line for a joyfull ride?
Each twist, each turn, brings colorful sight,
In the wildest of plans, take that flight!

The Power of Quiet Decisions

In the stillness of the night,
A choice must be made right.
Should I eat cake or pie,
The answer's always 'why?'

With whispers soft and sly,
I ponder, oh my, oh my!
The remote calls my name,
Is Netflix to blame for this game?

In the silence, I chuckle,
Advice turns to muckle.
A snack for every thought,
And in dreams, I am caught.

So I strategize with flair,
While lounging in my chair.
Decisions can be light,
Like snacks abandoned at night.

Gifted with Uncertainty

Morning coffee in hand,
A jazz band in my head.
What's for breakfast, you ask?
Maybe toast, or an affair with bread?

The calendar's a mess,
Every date screams 'guess!'
Will I dance or will I bake?
It's a mystery I'll undertake.

In the gym, I can't decide,
To lift weights or simply hide.
A workout's at my side,
It's either fitness or a ride!

So I flick the coin once more,
Flip and watch it soar.
What's next on my great quest?
With humor, I jest and jest.

Caught in a Whirlwind of Options

A menu with a thousand meals,
Do I want fish or steel wheels?
Spaghetti here, sushi there,
I'm spinning, oh I swear!

With options left and right,
Shall I soar or take flight?
A dress for a ball,
Or pajamas and a wall?

A thousand paths beckon me,
But which one sets me free?
In this chaos, I laugh loud,
As I dance in a cloud.

So I close my eyes and see,
What's best for just me.
In a whirlwind, I twirl,
Just another day in this whirl.

The Balance of Serenity and Chaos

In the quiet of my space,
Serenity's a lovely place.
But chaos gives a thrill,
So let's juggle with skill!

I light a candle's glow,
While planning my next show.
A peaceful tea I sip,
It's a balancing trip.

With laughter in the air,
I spill my drink with flair.
But the mess is half the fun,
So let chaos run!

In the end, I find my way,
Juggling night into day.
With giggles in between,
The best of both I've seen.

Shadows and Sunbeams

In the glow of morning light,
I tripped on my own two feet.
A shadow waved and said, "Hey there!"
The sun laughed, not missing a beat.

Chasing dreams like a squirrel on caffeine,
I fumbled and dropped my pretzel.
Life's a circus, I'm cracking jokes,
As I juggle around my vessel.

Pies in the sky, a thought so absurd,
I mixed up my cereal with fruit.
The breakfast gods let out a cheer,
Now my spoon feels fancy, to boot.

Embrace the quirk; it gives a flare,
When you smile while wearing a shoe.
The playground's a face, wide and free,
Now let's dance under skies so blue.

Scripting Destiny with Heart

With crayons in hand, I wrote my fate,
A color outside the lines.
I sketched my dreams on a napkin,
And ate half when hunger shines.

My fortune's nearer than a sneeze,
Each hiccup tells a tale untold.
I'm flipping pancakes of possibility,
With syrup as sweet as gold.

Wrote a symphony with claps and squeals,
My orchestra's a cat and a shoe.
The audience roars, my bow takes flight,
Never thought I'd conduct my own zoo.

A dance-off against my lazy dog,
I led with moves that were creative.
He flopped and snored; I waved goodbye,
Guess his rhythm was just not native.

The Mosaic of Experience

Life's a puzzle made of snacks,
Each piece a chip or a dip.
I dropped my talent in a bowl,
And spilled joy with every sip.

A patchwork quilt of crazy days,
Woven tight with laughter threads.
I stitched a smile on my sleeve,
While wearing mismatched beds!

With every fumble, a story blooms,
Like flowers sprouting from a shoe.
I stroll through gardens of oops and yay,
Each scent is something new.

Friends are the tiles in my design,
They crack me up, and that's the key.
Together we dance, paint splashed with flair,
Embracing each silly decree.

Embracing the Unknown

Peeking around life's twisty bends,
I find surprises waiting there.
Like socks that vanish in the wash,
Or shoes that just don't seem to pair.

When life gives lemons, I juggle bright,
With lemonade dreams in my sight.
I draw mustaches on frowning cows,
Giving bleats a comical plight.

Adventures wait like suspicious cats,
Whiskers twitching to ask me why.
I leap forward, then take two steps back,
As mysterious squirrels start to fly.

Data's mixed, and so am I,
With charts made of spaghetti strands.
Holding tight to each mistake,
With laughter, I navigate these lands.

The Colors of Your Path

Choose the hues that paint your day,
A splash of chaos, then ballet.
Green for mischief, blue for cheer,
As laughter dances, you persevere.

Crayons scattered, all around,
Each scribble holds a silly sound.
A little purple, a dash of red,
Mix them up—this is how you spread.

Step outside, don the silly hat,
Stomp the bushes, hold the cat.
Chase the shadows, twirl with zest,
In your own ring, you're the best!

So grab your brush and paint away,
Tomorrow's canvas starts today.
With every stroke, embrace the mix,
Create a world, a vibrant fix.

Dancing with Uncertainty

Waltz with doubt, it's quite a thrill,
Two left feet, but still you will.
Sway to the rhythm of your heart,
Even when you don't know where to start.

The floor's a mess, a wild junkyard,
Yet every twist leaves you charred.
Laughing at steps that seem absurd,
Each trip contributes to the word!

Count the beats of whimsy's tune,
As you tango under the moon.
Fumble forwards, slide and glide,
In this fun house, do not hide.

To dance is joy, embrace the fate,
Let the awkwardness serenade.
Spin into mishaps, grin with glee,
Every wrong step sets you free.

Echoes of Possibility

Whispers of what-might-be float,
Like a quirky little boat.
Sail on thoughts, jump into dreams,
Where everything's never as it seems.

Cackle loud at quirks unknown,
The wild twists, how they've grown.
Each echoing giggle sets you free,
In the maze of what you might decree.

What if unicorns tried to bake?
Or fishes danced with every shake?
Let imagination run and spark,
With options stretching far 'til dark.

So heed the call of chance and cheer,
For every riddle holds its dear.
Play the game, don't fear the mist,
Adventures wait upon your list.

Threads of Your Own Weaving

Gather threads from every laugh,
Slice through fears like a crafty half.
Stitch together joy and glee,
In the quilt that's uniquely free.

Patch the spots where knots might form,
Tangle dances keep you warm.
Each quirk a color, wildly bright,
Weaving tales of day and night.

Snag a stitch, unweave despair,
Flip the fabric, show you care.
From snags come patterns new and bold,
In the tapestry, watch it unfold.

So grab those threads, let's all create,
A playful journey, never late.
In every twist, make it your way,
Life's a yarn you get to sway.

Flourishing in Every Season

In winter's chill, I wear a frown,
But find a snowman in my gown.
Spring blooms bright, I'll dance with glee,
And bounce like bunnies, wild and free.

Summer's heat, oh what a joke,
Melting popsicles down my throat.
Autumn leaves like confetti fall,
Pumpkin spice, my favorite thrall.

With every season, quirks arise,
I chase the sun, then dodge the skies.
Laughing loud, I seize the day,
For every moment's here to play.

So here's my toast to life's grand blend,
Where every twist can be a friend.
With silly hats and jokes anew,
I make my way, and you can too.

A Sigh of Freedom

They say relax, just take it slow,
But my cup's full, it's time to go!
I trip on dreams, I dance on air,
With every mishap, I stop and stare.

A clumsy bird forgot to soar,
It flaps its wings, then drops to floor.
Yet here I am, without a care,
Laughing at life's tangled snare.

Freedom's weight can feel quite light,
Think half-full glass, it feels just right.
So let me tumble, let me roll,
With goofy moves that feed my soul.

I'll wear my smiles like funky hats,
While cat memes dance and joke like cats.
To sigh and chuckle is the key,
To living wild and feeling free.

Sculpting Dreams in the Soil of Today

With garden tools, I plant my hopes,
Twirling around like silly blobs.
A seedling sprouts, but what to grow?
A carrot? Or a dance show?

I water thoughts with laughter bright,
Weeds of worry take to flight.
In sunny rays, my mind will play,
Procrastination? That's the way!

Molding dreams in dirt and clay,
My fancy plans sometimes stray.
But with a giggle, I will find,
The wildest dreams are born unlined.

So dig and laugh, don't hide away,
For every blunder's here to stay.
With hands in soil, my heart will sway,
Crafting sunshine each new day.

The Mirror of Your Choices

A mirror's glance, what do I see?
A face that pulls funny faces at me.
With every choice, a cringe or cheer,
Am I wise or just a sheer deer?

I flip a coin, heads or tails,
Should I cook or mail my meals?
Spaghetti's great, but burns my top,
While takeout waits, oh what a flop!

Decisions dance, and I ensue,
With pizza place or fancy stew.
A life of swaps, like shuffling decks,
I play my hand, and earn the heck!

So laugh at mirrors, oh so bright,
Reflecting choices, wrong or right.
With every giggle, I will find,
A joyful twist that's one of a kind.

Emblems of Transformation

In a world where socks go missing,
A lone shoe waits, reminiscing.
Folded dreams in laundry piles,
Chasing hope with goofy smiles.

Butterflies flutter in their flight,
With secrets kept within their sight.
A caterpillar bakes a pie,
Wonders if it's time to fly.

Life's a puzzle, missing parts,
Origami swans and dancing hearts.
We patch the quilt of what we miss,
Always adding our own twist.

So don't you worry or feel stressed,
Just add sprinkles; do your best!
With every sip of rainbow tea,
You'll see how quirky life can be!

Waves of Hope

The surfboards crash with giggles loud,
Each wave fights hard to draw a crowd.
Seagulls dive for fries on the strand,
While sunblock greets the summer's hand.

A jellyfish winks, a sight most rare,
Serves lemonade with utmost flair.
Beach towels dance like champs in sun,
With flip-flops flying, oh what fun!

Dune rats share their popcorn stash,
While waves come in with quite the splash.
Hold tight to joy; ride through the sea,
In every swell, it's wild and free!

So build your castles with a grin,
And let the sandy laughter in.
With tides that change, just go with flow,
Embrace the quirks; let happiness grow!

The Dance of Intentions

In the garden, veggies prance,
Tomatoes sing a curious dance.
Carrots wear top hats with glee,
Radishes float on a green sea.

Bees buzz with a saucy flair,
Hip-hop pollinates through the air.
Cabbages twist, though shy they seem,
To savor dreams and build their team.

Whimsical thoughts in the twilight glow,
Do the cha-cha to the moon's show.
With every leaf that twirls about,
Life's a party—let's laugh and shout!

So plant your hopes with hearty cheer,
Even weeds can find their way here.
With every step on this grand stage,
Take a bow—this is your page!

Glimmers of Resilience

In a world of wobbling chairs,
We laugh at how a cat declares.
Life's ups and downs, a comical sway,
With each new tumble, find your way!

Toast your marshmallows, burn them right,
Giggling as they take to flight.
Lollipops drop from candy trees,
Worries vanish in a sweet breeze.

Socks on hands, we dance like fools,
Making magic, bending rules.
Through every glitch and every blip,
A little giggle gives life a flip!

So gather 'round and share your tale,
With laughter echoing like a gale.
In quirky moments, the heart finds bliss,
Resilience shines as we laugh like this!

Embracing Intention with Grace

I'm trying to set my goal, so bold,
But I trip on my own shoelaces of gold.
With coffee spilled on my new white shirt,
I laugh and think, 'Hey, this could hurt.'

Each plan I sketch becomes quite absurd,
Like teaching a cat to sing, how absurd!
But with each flop, I learn and grow,
And now I'm a pro at the circus show.

Waking up late, my day's off to a start,
With a breakfast of chaos, a true work of art.
I throw together socks of mismatched grace,
And strut like the queen of this wild, crazy place.

So here's to the journey, quirky and free,
With every misstep, I dance with glee.
Life's little hiccups are just part of the race,
I'll take it all in — with a smile on my face.

The Cartography of Inner Landscapes

I mapped my dreams on a napkin one night,
With crayons and coffee, it felt just right.
But when I drew oceans, I made it rain,
With jellybeans floating, what a silly gain!

I marked the mountains of things I would do,
But they ended up as a giant fondue.
Each journey I chart is filled with bright sun,
And unicorns dancing — oh, this could be fun!

Sometimes I stumble on paths made of cheese,
My plans turning wobbly, just like my knees.
Yet through each detour, I smile wide,
For who knows what wonders are waiting inside?

So grab a crayon, let's throw caution away,
Let the world be our map in this game we play.
In all of my journeys, chaos is bliss,
Adventures await in a land on my list.

Finding Beauty in the Mundane

I found a pearl in a pile of socks,
While hunting for treasures in my old box.
Dust bunnies danced with the thrill of delight,
As I laughed at the chaos, oh what a sight!

Each grocery trip, an expedition so grand,
With lists of mischief crafted by hand.
I dodged the carts like a ninja quite sly,
Picking up snacks like a sugar-crazed guy.

The toaster pops up, a symphony sweet,
While leftovers whisper and some like to greet.
I've baked a cake with a sprinkle of flair,
With a dash of forgetfulness, all's fair, I swear!

So I toast to the ordinary, what a grand treat,
Finding joy in the mundane under my feet.
Through spilled milk and mismatched towels,
I've learned to laugh at the world's playful growls.

A Kaleidoscope of Possibilities

I peek through my scope at a world full of cheer,
With possibilities bright, yet close to my beer.
I swirl and I twirl in this whimsical space,
As colors collide in a joyful embrace.

The clock ticks away, but who's counting time?
I danced with my coffee, felt oh-so-divine.
With socks on my hands, I created my fate,
Spinning around like I'm perfectly late.

Every mishap's a new adventure in sight,
From tripping on shoelaces to snowball fights.
A character sketch with broad strokes and a frown,
Ends up a masterpiece of silly and clown.

So let's shake our maracas and sing loud and clear,
With the world as our canvas, let's smear and smear.
In this kaleidoscope, there's joy at play,
Every twist and turn adds to our array.

The Art of Living Unscripted

Wake up and spill coffee on your shirt,
It's just a canvas for your day's alert.
Forget the plans, let spontaneity reign,
Dance through the rain, forget the mundane.

Grab a taco at three, why not indulge?
Life's a buffet, don't let it divulge.
Sing off-key in the shower, belt out a tune,
The world's your stage, make it a cartoon.

To-do lists can wait, let chaos preside,
Who needs a map? Let your whims be your guide.
Run towards the ice cream, embrace the delight,
Savor each scoop, with laughter ignite.

So here's to the mess, let your quirks shine bright,
In the art of living, you're the lead in the light.
Strike up a pose, give a wink to the stars,
Unscripted giggles, that's how you raise bars.

Whispers in the Wind

Caught in a breeze, my hat takes a flight,
Chasing it down, what a comical sight!
Laughter erupts as I stumble and sway,
The wind makes me dance, come what may.

Conversations with squirrels, they chatter a lot,
What wisdom they share, but I miss every thought.
They scurry away with a flick of their tails,
While I ponder my choices and laugh at my fails.

Clouds above me are giggling too,
Why stress the small stuff? They've got nothing to do.
Fill up your days with whimsical cheer,
Even the sun seems to waltz, my dear.

So let nature's whispers guide your quest,
In this odd little journey, just be your best.
Pick up a dandelion, blow wishes to sky,
And remember, the giggles are what's truly spry.

A Canvas of Tomorrow

Pour out the paint, let colors collide,
Each brushstroke a whisper, let laughter reside.
Smudged edges and splatters, a masterpiece bright,
Life's a canvas to fill, not a wall for a fight.

Pick orange for mornings, a splash of pure glee,
Mix purple with hope, it's as wild as can be.
Dip in the blues when the mood's feeling dreary,
With each chaotic dab, say goodbye to the weary.

Sketch out your dreams, even the silliest kind,
Stick figure adventures, they're never maligned.
A piñata of wishes to bash with a grin,
Embrace every color, let the fun begin.

So laugh at the mess, it's what makes you whole,
Your canvas is waiting, let funny take control.
In shades of tomorrow, create and ignite,
A joyful explosion, let laughter take flight.

Moments Weaved in Gold

In pockets of time, find treasures galore,
A sunbeam that tickles, a friend at your door.
Moments are threads in a tapestry spun,
Each giggle and smile, a stitch on the run.

Stumble on puddles, splash a bit wide,
Why walk when you can take a fun, rainy slide?
Jump into joy, let your heart be the guide,
The simple absurdities are where we abide.

Daydreams in colors that bounce off the wall,
Knowing tomorrow is just another call.
Embrace all the quirks that make you unique,
In a world quite bonkers, it's fun we seek.

So gather those moments, weave them with care,
In gold threads of laughter, let them declare.
To bloom with a jest, feel the sparkle unfold,
In this wacky journey, find your moments of gold.

Sketches of a Dreamer

With a crayon in hand, I doodle and play,
My cat's the muse, in a fanciful way.
She twirls like a dancer, under moonlight's beam,
And I'm just the artist, lost in a dream.

Coffee and pastries, breakfast in bed,
Who says you can't feast when you envision a spread?
I paint my own sunshine, no clouds up above,
Sipping on joy, the flavor of love.

A paper boat floats, on a puddle it laughs,
While my sock collection performs the best half.
Tickles from rainbows, light-hearted and bold,
The world can be silly, if you just let it unfold.

So twirl like a dervish, let laughter ignite,
In the sketches we make, everything feels right.
Playful as children, in a world of delight,
With crayons and dreams, painting life into sight.

Echoes of Resilience

In the face of a grouch, I pull out my grin,
Like a rubber band, it snaps back again.
I juggle my worries, like balls in the air,
And giggle at problems that don't seem quite fair.

Life tosses curveballs, I catch them with cheer,
With a wink and a nudge, I've got nada to fear.
Caffeine-fueled laughter spills over the brim,
As I dance through the chaos, on a whim.

Resilience, my buddy, always by my side,
With a sassy remark, we take on the ride.
In the garden of mishaps, we plant our own seeds,
With a side of absurdity, we grow funny deeds.

So bring on the lemons, I'll mix them with glee,
Make some zingy good lemonade, just wait and see.
In the circus of life, I'll juggle and cheer,
With echoes of laughter, I'll conquer the year.

Embracing the Unsung

A whisper from shadows, an ode to the new,
In a world of the overlooked, I find my own crew.
With the broomstick and mop, we dance through the night,
Making magic from chores, in our carefree flight.

Here's to the quiet, the ones who persist,
While we pop balloons, and create an uproarious twist.
With giggles and chuckles, we march to our song,
In the realm of the unsung, we all can belong.

So paint me a story, in colors so wild,
With unicorn dreams and the heart of a child.
Let's flip through the pages of those who are shy,
As we weave threads of joy, beneath a bright sky.

In the laughter of gatherings, embrace what is true,
In the simplicity found, it's remarkably new.
Together we stumble, yet grow through the fun,
In the dance of the quirky, we outshine the sun.

A Palette of Perceptions

Life's a canvas splashed with paint and hot mess,
I'll dip my brush, and wear my own dress.
With tickles of teal and a splash of bright red,
I'll color outside lines where the adventure had led.

With a palette of laughter, I'll stir up the light,
A picture of whimsy, oh what a sight!
Let's sprinkle confetti on doubts and regrets,
Creating a masterpiece of hopes and sunsets.

Every flop is a flourish, don't try to retract,
For art's in the chaos; that's simply a fact.
I'll dance with the brush, in a rhythm so grand,
As I splash on the canvas with spontaneous hand.

So let's toast to the colors, bold brushes of chance,
In a mosaic of madness, let's give life a dance.
With humor as our paint, we'll be artists divine,
In this unfinished gallery, our spark will still shine.

Threads of Self-Discovery

In a room full of mirrors, I'd dance with glee,
Waving to the stranger who looks just like me.
Stitching my quirks with a thread of delight,
Every patch tells a tale, oh what a sight!

With wobbly steps, I adjust my own crown,
Trip on my laces, then grin, not frown.
Every misstep, a giggle, a twirl,
Embracing the moments that make my heart whirl.

In the fabric of days, I weave and I mend,
Finding my style as I twist and I bend.
A pattern emerges, quirky and bright,
A tapestry of laughs and the funny insights.

So here I stand, with my patchwork of cheer,
Learning to savor each wonderful year.
With threads of my choices, so vibrant and free,
I craft a wild story, and oh, it's just me!

The Palette of Emotions

With crayons and chaos, I splash and I play,
Mixing up feelings in a colorful way.
A drizzle of joy and a splash of surprise,
Life's a wild canvas, let's color the skies!

A dab of confusion, a stroke of blue mad,
Throw in some laughter, it's not all so bad.
Paintbrush in hand, I create my own tune,
Ballet of feelings beneath a bright moon.

In this whimsical world, I swirl and I spin,
Wrestling my thoughts, let the fun begin!
Each shade and each hue tells a story so bright,
An artist of moments, I'll sketch them with light.

So let's hold our brushes, embrace all the feels,
With giggles and splatters, it's truth that reveals.
In this palette of chaos, there's beauty, you see,
A masterpiece crafted—my own symphony!

The Poetry of Each Step

With feet that are tap dancing, I take to the street,
Writing my story with every small beat.
Each shuffle and stomp is a quirky refrain,
A rhythm of moments that dance through the rain.

Every wobble and jig, a word on the floor,
Spinning in circles, then leaping for more.
Stomping on puddles, I laugh out loud,
Each step is a stanza, a joy I'll expound.

From stumbles to jiggles, I'm crafting my prose,
Bouncing through life, where the airflow just goes.
With every odd shuffle, I pen my own verse,
Life's a grand poem, for better or worse.

So join in the dance, don't just sit still,
Life's rhythm is funny, a whimsical thrill.
With each step I take, I'm not out of luck,
For in each little twirl, I've found my own chuck!

The Compass of a Curious Heart

With my compass in hand, I wander the scene,
Chasing the squirrels, I'm not too serene.
North, south, east, or wherever they dart,
Every little adventure is a kick in my heart.

Through fields of blue daisies and hills made of green,
I stumble and tumble, a sight to be seen.
With questions like arrows, I shoot for the stars,
Who knew a detour could lead to new bars?

With laughter as fuel, I roam without fear,
A curious heart is the best souvenir.
I follow my whims, where they may lead,
Eagerly sowing a joy-filled seed.

So here's to the journeys that twist and they turn,
With a grin and a giggle, it's my soul that will yearn.
A compass unsteady may point to the fun,
With a curious spirit, the adventure's begun!

The Alchemy of Choice

In a world of dreams and whims,
Where ice cream wins over gym.
Choose your toppings, make them bold,
Life's a sundae, or so I'm told.

Pick a path, wear mismatched socks,
Dance like nobody checks your clocks.
Craft a tale, weave in some glee,
A chuckle here, just let it be.

What's a goal? Just pick a snack,
With every bite, you'll find your track.
Success is just a funky dance,
So cha-cha-cha, give it a chance!

In this circus, juggle time,
Silly clowns will be your rhyme.
Squeeze some laughs from everyday,
With simple joys, you'll lead the way.

Cradled by the Present

Gathered here in this cozy nook,
With coffee cups and a favorite book.
Forget the future, it can wait,
Why not indulge? Just call it fate!

Tickle your toes, let laughter burst,
Revel in moments, every thirst.
The clock's a joker, wearing a grin,
So eat that cake, just dig right in!

Life is playful, a cat with string,
Each little moment wears a crown and bling.
Slip on those shoes that squeak and squawk,
Join the parade, let your joy unlock!

Hide-and-seek with time is grand,
Chase the sun, just grab its hand.
Embrace the now; it's all in good fun,
With giggles, dances, we're never done!

A Mirrored Reflection

Staring back is that quirky grin,
Who knew my best friend lived within?
A detective wearing silly hats,
Chasing dreams like whimsical cats.

Bounce into life with a mouthful of cheer,
Scoop up the glitter, make it your sphere.
Each mistake a dance, a costumed affair,
Waltzing with fate like you just don't care!

Flip a coin, see what it says,
Heads, take a nap; tails, it's a craze!
Who knew the secret? It's jest and play,
In this show, we're stars, come what may!

With a wink and a laugh, take a bow,
In this grand mirror, I see the now.
Life's a riddle, a puzzle, a game,
So join the fun, there's no need for shame!

Carving Purpose from Pebbles

In a garden filled with stones and grime,
I found a marvel, a treasure in time.
Carve a smile on each little rock,
Life's not a clock, it's a whimsical clock!

Skip a pebble, hear it splash,
With each rippling laugh, make a dash.
Create a sculpture, let spirits soar,
Every chip a memory, a playful score.

Hustle and bustle? Nah, take it slow,
Let your worries be carried by flow.
Breathe in the fun, exhale the stress,
Every day's a doodle, just draw your best!

So gather your stones, make a stack,
A monument of joy, flair for the lack.
With a wink to the sky, take a stand,
In this quirky art, we all understand!

The Balance of Being

In the circus of dreams, I juggle my schemes,
A tightrope of whims, or so it seems.
My kitten is coaching, with paws in the air,
While I tumble and fumble, without a care.

With coffee as fuel, I trip on my fate,
As my sock and my shoe conspire to mate.
Each step is a dance, a clumsy ballet,
I laugh at my mess, it's just another day.

The world spins around in a top hat and tie,
As I toss all my worries up to the sky.
Who knew being human was quite this absurd?
I'll take my sweet time, while my voice goes unheard.

So here's to the whims of this fanciful ride,
With giggles to share and no place to hide.
Embrace the delight of the zany and wild,
For in every mishap, there's always a smile.

Journey Through Uncharted Waters

Set sail on a whim in a boat made of cheese,
With seagulls and squirrels, I laugh with the breeze.
The compass is broken, but why should I care?
I'm surfing through chaos, it's quite a sweet affair.

An octopus dances, all eight arms in sync,
While I sip on the ocean, that's oddly pink.
The treasure I seek is a giggle or two,
As I splash through the waves in my mismatched shoe.

With each turn of the tide, I'm swept up in fun,
While dolphins write poems under the sun.
I'm lost in the shuffle of foam and delight,
Not searching for maps, just some stars in the night.

So here's to the frolic where worries don't dwell,
In waters uncharted, I'm under a spell.
With laughter my anchor, I'll float ever free,
Embracing the wobbles, just you wait and see.

Sentences of Hope

In the book of my days, I scribble in crayon,
With plot twists and giggles, I'm never alone.
Each chapter unfolds with a wink and a cheer,
While punctuation dances, and spelling's sincere.

The comma is winking, the period grins,
As my verb starts to frolic and twirl with the sins.
In margins, I doodle my dreams that spill over,
With rainbows and unicorns, I'm searching for clover.

Adventures in footnotes, and puns in the text,
Where laughter is golden and never perplexed.
With every new sentence, I weave my own tale,
A story of hope where the humor won't fail.

So write me a script that dances like stars,
In the book of tomorrow, we'll dodge all the cars.
With giggles as chapters, and love as the plot,
I'll pen out my wonders, and give it a shot.

The Canvas of Now

Splashing my thoughts onto canvas so bright,
With colors that giggle, they dance in the light.
Some dots and some dashes, a squiggle or two,
Each stroke tells a story, a pie with no rue.

The palette is messy, and so are my hands,
As laughter drips slowly from whimsical bands.
I'm painting my worries, with smiles so large,
Every hue has a story, I smile at the charge.

With a twist of the brush, I let my heart roam,
In this gallery, I find that I'm home.
No pressure to follow, no outline to trace,
Just me and my colors, in this joyful space.

So here's to the moments that splash and collide,
With whimsy and wonder, let's take it in stride.
The canvas is waiting, so come take a peek,
It's painted with laughter, it's vibrant and chic.

Harmony in Dissonance

In the chaos of socks, I find my flair,
Juggling coffee cups, it's how I dare.
My cat's a ninja, she runs up the wall,
Embracing mishaps, I answer the call.

Spilled beans dance like jazz in the air,
Waltzing with worries that just aren't there.
With mismatched shoes, I strut down the street,
Finding my rhythm in every heartbeat.

The toaster's my muse, it burns with style,
I'll toast my failures, wear them with a smile.
In this symphony of quirky delight,
I laugh with the shadows, I'm feeling light.

Melodies twist with the clang of my life,
Chasing after chaos, I run with a knife.
In the dissonance, I find my tune,
Just laugh with the mess and dance with the moon.

The Ethereal Pathway

Floating on clouds of cereal haze,
My morning routine blurs the mundane days.
Slippers are jetpacks, they zoom me ahead,
In a world made of marshmallows, I'm never misled.

Starry-eyed dreams in the afternoon sun,
Cereal for dinner? Oh boy, that's fun!
Why fret over details that cloud my good cheer?
I'll wear a sombrero and drink my root beer.

Sidewalk surfboards and paper-clip sails,
In my kingdom of laughter, there's no room for fails.
In the land of the odd, I take every leap,
Painting my pathway in colors so deep.

Giggles echo in each twist I invoke,
Life's a whimsical dance, come join in the stroke.
Steering through oddity, my spirit will soar,
Riding this highway where fun's never a bore.

Radiance Born from Attitude

With a wink to the mirror, I queue up my grin,
Shiny and sparkly, let the fun begin!
The hairbrush my wand, I cast spells with glee,
Unicorns dance as I sip my hot tea.

I wear my confidence like a bright neon suit,
Kicking nonsense away, oh what's so astute!
Every stutter, a giggle, every trip, a jest,
I'm the king of my castle, I'm simply the best.

A smile like sunshine on a cloudy old morn,
I'll strut through the chaos, reborn and adorned.
The world's my stage, and I'm stealing the show,
Radiating laughter, just basking in glow.

In this carnival tent of quirks and odd bits,
I flip the script, life's a stack of good hits.
With a chuckle and twirl, I embrace the road game,
My attitude sparkles, there's joy to reclaim.

A Journey through the Ordinary

Amidst the pile of laundry, a treasure we find,
A sock with a smile, I know it's quite kind.
I trip on my shoelace, it's part of the act,
Swaying like a leaf, it's my comedy pact.

The garden's my stage with weeds as the cast,
Each flower a jester, they bloom unsurpassed.
With every dull chore comes a wink and a grin,
I'm pirouetting dust bunnies, let the fun begin!

I'll ride on my broomstick of bills overdue,
Dressed as a pirate, with dreams that come true.
Each mundane moment, a chance to ensue,
Sing jolly tunes as the yard turn to dew.

In the art of the simple, I find my delight,
Each cookie jar adventure, a whimsical bite.
I'll stroll through the ordinary, dancing with flair,
Finding gold in the common, in laughter we share.

Tides of the Heart

Oh, the waves crash hard, then gently sway,
Like my big plans that never stay.
I build my castles, they sink with a laugh,
But hey, I still got my cozy craft!

A surfboard ride on a sea of glee,
With jellyfish friends, and tea for three.
Got a floatie shaped like a rubber duck,
Every wave a twist, yet I feel so stuck!

Catch me sunbathing under the stars,
In a life where we drive invisible cars.
Each hiccup a dance, a jig of delight,
Who needs a manual on how to be right?

So splash, dive deep, and take a chance,
In this quirky ocean of goofy romance.
With laughter as my buoy, I'll ride the tide,
For in this fun mayhem, I'll surely glide!

Unwritten Stanzas

In a book that's blank, I start to scribble,
Where rhymes get wobbly and words start to giggle.
Each page a giant game of charades,
With metaphors tangled in silly cascades.

The plot thickens like gravy on toast,
Characters dancing, doing the most.
There's a cat playing chess, oh what a scene,
In this whimsical world, I reign as queen!

As I pen down the zany, my pen plays a tune,
A symphony crafted beneath the round moon.
With coffee spills and a donut on hand,
I write my adventure, oh isn't it grand?

So let's craft some tales, with giggles en masse,
From the silliest moments, let's raise a glass!
For unwritten stanzas are where we belong,
In this book of mischief, come join along!

Footprints of a Dreamer

With flip-flops on, I stroll through the sand,
Making wild shapes like a doodling hand.
A pizza slice here, a rocket ship there,
Each footprint a wish, floating in the air.

The seagulls chuckle as I trip and fall,
Inventing excuses, I laugh through it all.
A splash of the ocean, a tickle of foam,
In the land of the silly, I've found my home!

Clouds above me take whimsical forms,
Like cotton candy during bizarre storms.
With every step, I dance with delight,
In a world where the weird feels perfectly right!

As stars twinkle down, and dreams start to swirl,
I sketch out my footprints, watch them unfurl.
For a dreamer's journey has laughs in the seams,
In a silly parade of outrageous dreams!

Penned with a Gentle Hand

With every stroke, my pen does prance,
Creating a story that shimmies and dances.
Letters all twirl like ballerinas in air,
As I scribble my hopes, without any care.

A cat in a top hat writing a tale,
With a sidekick mouse, on a miniature sail.
Together they sail through pastry and pie,
In this silly world where giggles fly high.

The ink spills like laughter, just dripping with cheer,
Each page a treasure where whimsy is clear.
Dancing clouds, magic socks in a whirl,
I scripted a circus with an acrobat girl!

So let's pen our stories, with joy in our grip,
Adventure awaits on this wild little trip.
With a gentle touch, let your heart unleash,
For in every word, there's a moment of peace!

Crafting Reality's Canvas

With crayons in hand, we sketch our fate,
A splash of blue, a swirl of bait.
The cats take over, the dog strikes a pose,
Amidst all the chaos, who knows how it goes?

We dangle our dreams on a crooked line,
Dance with our worries, sip bubble-free wine.
Perhaps we'll fly, or trip on a shoe,
But hey, what's an adventure without something to rue?

A sprinkle of laughter, a dash of the weird,
Inventing the normal, by now we're well-acquired.
With every new morning, we twist and we bend,
Making our masterpiece, no start and no end.

So grab your supplies, let's start with a grin,
Paint outside the edges, feel the rush within.
Reality's canvas, uneven but bright,
We're all just artists, creating delight!

The Art of Becoming

Step right up, the show begins,
Juggling dreams, while tied in sins.
The acrobat winks, the tightrope shakes,
Just hold your breath, for heaven's sakes!

Life's a buffet, where choices abound,
Picking tricky dishes, some lost, some found.
A sprinkle of chaos, a whip of absurd,
Each bite's an adventure, sounds utterly stirred!

We paint our oddities with shades of thrill,
A dash of mishaps, a twist of will.
Sometimes we tumble, sometimes we soar,
Every wobble shapes us, and adds to the lore.

So grab your paintbrush and don your best hat,
Between jests and jigs, let's have a good chat.
Becoming our canvas, with colors so bright,
The art is in trying; oh, what a sight!

In the Hands of Tomorrow

Tick-tock, little clock, what do you see?
Tomorrow's a mystery, dancing with glee.
Will it gift us a dance, or just serve us tea?
Let's hope it's a rollercoaster, not calculus, whee!

With sandwiches packed, laughter in tow,
We skip into fields where wildflowers grow.
Trusting the future, but packing some fun,
Expecting the absurd, until day is done.

Fate wears a hat, bright pink and quite round,
It's mostly just silly, but oh, how profound!
With wiggles and chuckles, we wander and roam,
Tomorrow's a stage where we all find a home.

Let's launch paper rockets and shout without end,
With each ticking second, let joy be our friend.
In the hands of tomorrow, so wacky, so bright,
Together we'll twirl in the dance of delight!

Chasing Shadows

In the park, I chase my shadow,
He's quick and laughs, 'Let's take it slow!'
Sprints to the trees, then hides in the light,
Catching a glimmer is quite the delight!

We play tag with the clouds, lost in the day,
Twisting and tumbling, in a whimsical way.
My shadow's a rascal, he leaps and he bounds,
But I'll catch him yet, in the laughter that sounds.

We throw popcorn at pigeons, and giggle aloud,
My shadow's the jester; oh, isn't he proud?
Each moment a jest, each blink a surprise,
In this chase of the silly, we dance in the skies.

So let's shake off our worries, and join in the fun,
Every shadow's a partner until we're all done.
Chasing the laughter, and cheering the dawn,
In a light-hearted race, the silliness shone.

Embracing Light

Glowing bright, the sun's quite a sight,
It chuckles and beams, blending day with night.
With arms open wide, we bask in its glow,
Forget all the weight, let the worries go slow.

With each golden ray, we dance with delight,
Pirouettes and twirls, oh what a height!
Sunshine confetti falls down from above,
Sprinkling our moments with pockets of love.

As dusk starts to whisper, the stars make their play,
They twinkle like fireflies, lighting the way.
Soft shadows creep in, but don't you lose sight,
For the laughter we cherish helps us through the night.

So come on, my friend, let's chase off the gloom,
With giggles and grins, let our hearts burst and bloom.
Embracing the shimmer in all we ignite,
We're painting the future, with color and light!

In the Workshop of Time

In the workshop of time, we all have our tools,
Some carve out the dreams, while others play fools.
With a hammer of laughter and a chisel of cheer,
We build mighty wonders, or at least a good beer.

The clock ticks away as we fumble and dance,
With each blunder we make, we give fate a chance.
We paint over our mishaps with bright splashes of fun,
And toast to the chaos when the day's finally done.

So grab your old toolbox, it's all in good jest,
You might find a treasure or a hole in your chest.
Maybe it's laughter that crafts our grand fate,
Or simply a cake that we all can debate.

In the workshop of time, let your whimsy unfold,
Craft moments with giggles, let humor be bold.
For the messes we make in this workshop divine,
Are the sparks of our joy, the true gold of the line.

Navigating the Undefined

We're sailing on waters both murky and bright,
Navigating riddles under moon's quirky light.
With a map made of giggles and a compass of quirks,
We'll chart out our course and embrace all the jerks.

The waves may be bumpy, the seagulls may squawk,
But with laughter as wind, we'll take every block.
Each splash of the wave is a slap on the back,
A reminder that fun is the treasure we lack.

We'll dodge every thunder, we'll surf every breeze,
Waving flags of silliness, doing just as we please.
Every detour we take might just lead to delight,
In this nautical nonsense, let's bask in the sight.

So bring on the storms and the skies filled with gloom,
We'll dance in the rain while the whole world goes vroom!
In our ship made of laughter, we'll sail any sea,
For the undefined journey is just you and me!

The Sweetness of Small Moments

In the sweetness of small moments, we find our delight,
Like a puppy's first bark or a star shining bright.
A warm slice of pizza, the smell of the breeze,
These tiny sweet treasures are what truly appease.

A wink from a stranger, a dance in the rain,
Collecting these gems is never a pain.
With giggles afloat, we embrace the mundane,
And toast to the silly, for it's never in vain.

The warmth of that smile, the crunch of some chips,
A tickle of laughter that plays on our lips.
Each small moment cherished becomes a grand feast,
In a banquet of giggles, we savor the least.

So let's cherish the sunbeams and joys that we find,
For in tiny delights, we're blissfully blind.
In the sweetness of small moments, we thrive and we play,
For these are the riches that brighten our day!

Sketches of a Heartfelt Pursuit

In sketches of life, with crayons and glee,
We draw our adventures, come play along, see?
A heart with some scribbles, a smile full of ink,
In the gallery of chuckles, we pause just to think.

With brushes of kindness and paints of pure fun,
We create our own masterpiece, all on the run.
Each stroke tells a story of folly and cheer,
In this artful pursuit, there's nothing to fear.

From splashes of color to lines that run wild,
We sketch out the moments, where chaos is mild.
In each little misstep, a lesson is found,
With laughter as our canvas, we're joyfully bound.

So pick up your pencils and bring forth a grin,
In the sketches of life, let the fun truly begin.
For every small doodle is a heartfelt decree,
That joy lives in art, wild and fancy-free!

www.ingramcontent.com/pod-product-compliance
Lightning Source LLC
Chambersburg PA
CBHW051638160426
43209CB00004B/697